# BACON
# BEANS
# and BEER

# BACON
# BEANS
#  BEER

## ELIZA CROSS

PHOTOGRAPHS BY SUSAN BARNSON HAYWARD

GIBBS SMITH
TO ENRICH AND INSPIRE HUMANKIND

First Edition
25 24 23 22      8 7 6 5 4

Text © 2018 Eliza Cross
Photographs © 2018 Susan Barnson Hayward

Published by
Gibbs Smith
P.O. Box 667
Layton, Utah 84041

1.800.835.4993 orders
www.gibbs-smith.com

Designed by Sheryl Dickert
Food Styling by Corrine Miller

Printed and bound in China

Gibbs Smith books are printed on either recycled, 100% post-consumer waste, FSC-certified papers or on paper produced from sustainable PEFC-certified forest/controlled wood source. Learn more at www.pefc.org.

Library of Congress Cataloging-in-Publication Data

Names: Cross, Eliza, author.
Title: Bacon, beans and beer / Eliza Cross.
Description: Layton, Utah : Gibbs Smith, [2018] | Includes index.
Identifiers: LCCN 2018001264 | ISBN 9781423650409 (hardcover)
Subjects: LCSH: Cooking (Bacon) | Cooking (Beans) | Cooking (Beer) |
LCGFT:
  Cookbooks.
Classification: LCC TX749.5.P67 B32 2018 | DDC 641.3/6--dc23
LC record available at https://lccn.loc.gov/2018001264

# CONTENTS

# INTRODUCTION

Crispy, crunchy bacon. Tender, creamy beans. Bubbly, refreshing beer. Individually, they're three of the world's most palate-pleasing tastes. Pair them together, and the sum of their parts creates culinary magic. Appetizers, dinners, soups, salads, sides, sandwiches, and even sweets are transformed by the smoky, earthy, hoppy flavors of bacon, beans, and beer.

Savor the hearty pleasure of Pork Lovers' Maple Baked Beans (page 102). Delight in the slow-cooked goodness of Ale Caramelized Onion and Bacon Dip (page 22). Indulge in the succulent flavors of cheesy Bacon Crab Melts (page 62), and end your meal with a sweet treat like Bacon Bread Pudding drizzled with Vanilla Sauce (page 113).

The perfect accompaniment to any of these dishes is a glass of your favorite brew, and Beer Pairing Tips (see page 11) provide full gustatory guidance. Whether you prefer a crisp pilsner that perfectly complements a rich dish like Beer Bacon Mac and Cheese (page 68), or a dark, creamy stout that brings out the cocoa notes in Chocolate-Glazed Bacon Brownies (page 118), you're sure to find the ultimate match.

With simple preparations highlighting the honest flavors of "the three Bs," this collection of sixty-five beguiling recipes is guaranteed to wake up all of your taste buds.

# HELPFUL HINTS

## Makin' Bacon

Regular sliced bacon is generally about $1/16$ inch thick, and an average pound contains 16 to 20 slices. A pound of thick-sliced bacon is about $1/8$ inch thick and contains 12 to 16 slices per pound. The recipes in this book call for regular sliced bacon unless otherwise indicated.

Nitrate-free bacon is sometimes slightly saltier than regular bacon due to processing. Adjust salt accordingly if using nitrate-free bacon for the recipes in this book.

For an easy, mess-proof method of cooking bacon, arrange the slices on a broiler pan and bake in a preheated 350 degree oven to desired crispness, about 15–20 minutes.

## Bean Cuisine

For most beans, 1 pound dried beans equals 2 cups dried beans, which equals 5 to 6 cups of cooked beans.

A 15-ounce can of beans is slightly less than 2 cups of beans, so substitute $1\,7/8$ cups of cooked beans for 1 can. One pound of dried beans will yield roughly the equivalent of 3 (15-ounce) cans of beans.

## Cooking with Beer

Nonalcoholic, low alcohol (3.2%), and light (low calorie) beers can be substituted for regular beer in many recipes, but the beer flavor may be less pronounced.

When adding beer to a mixture, allow plenty of room in the pot or bowl since beer can foam up upon contact with other ingredients.

When cooking with very bitter beers, adding a touch of brown sugar, maple syrup, or honey may help balance the flavors.

When cooking with alcoholic beer, some alcohol may remain in the dish. In general, the longer a dish is cooked, the less alcohol that remains.

Because even small amounts of alcohol can be a problem for some people, advise guests if a dish has been prepared with beer.

# BEER PAIRING TIPS

Each beer type has a distinctive flavor profile that can enhance and compliment many cuisines. Keep these suggestions in mind when matching brews and food, and remember the best combination is the one that tastes good to you.

**PILSNER** is a crisp lager with a lightly bitter flavor. Enjoy it with rich foods like macaroni and cheese, or creamy soups like corn chowder.

**BOCK BEER** is a strong, darker lager with malty flavors. It pairs well with spicy foods like chicken wings or chili.

**WHEAT BEER** is often unfiltered, with a mellow, fruity flavor. Try it with lighter foods like salads or a Bacon and Shrimp Po' Boy (page 61).

**PALE ALE** is crisp, with a bitter, hoppy flavor. Enjoy it with Bacon-Wrapped Cheese Dogs (page 58), Bacon Cheese Fries (page 31), or Tex-Mex White Chili (page 52).

**IPA AND DOUBLE IPAS** are bitter, with more aggressive hops and malt flavors that pair well with spicy cuisine like red chili and hot wings.

**AMBER ALE** is a darker beer with caramel and medium bitter flavors. Enjoy it with barbecued ribs or Bacon Cheeseburger Meatloaf (page 76).

**PORTER** is a dark, medium-bodied beer with malty sweet and bitter hops flavors. Try it with roasted chicken and burgers.

**STOUT** is a dark, heavy beer with toasty coffee and malt flavors. Enjoy it with savory dishes like Beer and Bacon Beef Stew (page 44) and rich chocolate desserts.

# APPETIZERS
## and SNACKS

# BEER CANDIED BACON

**MAKES 6 SERVINGS**

1/3 cup regular or nonalcoholic beer

1/4 cup packed dark brown sugar

1/4 cup maple syrup

1 pound thick-cut bacon

2 teaspoons pepper

Preheat oven to 400 degrees. Line a rimmed baking sheet with aluminum foil.

Combine beer, sugar, and syrup in a small bowl, whisking well to dissolve sugar; set aside.

Arrange the bacon on baking sheet, overlapping if necessary. Place in oven and bake for 10 minutes. Reduce oven temperature to 275 degrees, remove pan from oven, and blot the rendered fat from the bacon with a paper towel.

Brush both sides of each strip of bacon with the beer syrup. Return to oven and bake for 10 minutes. Remove from oven and brush both sides with syrup. Turn bacon over and bake for 10 minutes. Remove from oven, brush both sides with syrup and sprinkle with pepper. Turn bacon over and bake until crispy and browned, about 8 minutes. Remove from oven and cool for 10 minutes before serving.

# BACON BEER CHEESE DIP

**MAKES ABOUT 3 1/2 CUPS**

1 (8-ounce) package cream cheese, softened

1 cup sour cream

1/3 cup regular or nonalcoholic beer

1 (1-ounce) envelope ranch salad dressing mix

2 cups grated cheddar cheese

6 strips bacon, cooked and finely crumbled

Pretzels, corn chips, or pita chips

In a large bowl, beat the cream cheese, sour cream, beer, and dressing mix together until smooth. Stir in the cheddar cheese and bacon and mix thoroughly to combine. Serve with pretzels, corn chips, or pita chips.

# CRISPY BEER CHICKEN WINGS

**MAKES 6 SERVINGS**

1 tablespoon packed brown sugar

1 tablespoon salt

1 (12-ounce) can or bottle beer

2 pounds chicken wings

1/4 cup butter

1/4 cup hot pepper sauce

2 teaspoons cornstarch

1 1/2 teaspoons garlic powder

1 1/2 teaspoons onion powder

1 1/2 teaspoons paprika

1/4 teaspoon cayenne pepper

2/3 cup blue cheese dressing

Preheat oven to 350 degrees. Line a baking sheet with aluminum foil and spray lightly with nonstick cooking spray.

In a large bowl, add the sugar, salt, and beer; whisk well to combine and dissolve sugar. Add chicken wings and toss gently to coat. Cover and refrigerate for 1 hour.

In a small saucepan, melt the butter. In a small bowl, whisk together the hot sauce and cornstarch. Add to the butter and whisk to combine. Heat to a simmer, remove from heat and set aside.

In a large ziplock bag, combine the garlic powder, onion powder, paprika, and cayenne. Remove wings from beer mixture and pat dry with paper towels; discard beer mixture. Add wings to bag with seasonings and shake until evenly coated. Arrange on baking sheet and pour hot sauce mixture evenly over wings. Bake for 30–35 minutes, or until an instant read thermometer registers 165 degrees on thickest part of chicken. Serve with blue cheese dressing.

# CHICKEN and BEAN QUESADILLAS

MAKES 24 APPETIZERS

1 tablespoon vegetable oil

1 small onion, finely chopped

1 pound boneless, skinless chicken breasts, cut in 1 x 1/2-inch strips

1 (11-ounce) can corn with red and green peppers, drained

1 teaspoon chili powder

1/2 teaspoon ground cumin

1/2 teaspoon salt

1/4 teaspoon pepper

8 (8-inch) flour tortillas

1 (15-ounce) can refried beans, divided

1 1/2 cups grated Mexican blend cheese

4 tablespoons butter, divided

2/3 cup sour cream

In a large frying pan, heat the oil over medium-high heat and cook the onion until translucent, about 5 minutes. Add the chicken and cook, stirring occasionally, until lightly browned and cooked through. Add the corn, chili powder, cumin, salt, and pepper and cook for 1 minute.

Spread 4 tortillas with 1/4 cup refried beans (reserve remaining beans for another use), and divide the chicken mixture among the tortillas. Divide the cheese evenly between the tortillas, sprinkling over top. Top with the remaining tortillas and press down gently.

Melt 1/2 tablespoon of butter in large frying pan or griddle over medium heat and cook the first quesadilla until golden brown. Lift the quesadilla with a large spatula, add another 1/2 tablespoon butter to the pan to melt. Carefully flip the quesadilla and cook the other side until golden brown. Repeat with remaining tortillas. Cut each quesadilla into 6 wedges and serve warm with sour cream.

# BACON-WRAPPED HONEY-SRIRACHA SCALLOPS

**MAKES 15 TO 20 APPETIZERS**

2 tablespoons honey

2 teaspoons Sriracha sauce

2 teaspoons olive oil

1 pound (15-20 count) fresh or frozen (thawed) sea scallops, rinsed and patted dry

1/2 pound thinly sliced bacon, halved crosswise

To make the glaze, whisk together the honey, Sriracha, and oil in a small bowl; set aside.*

Wrap each scallop with a half slice of bacon and secure with a toothpick.**

Preheat oven broiler. Line a baking sheet with aluminum foil. Arrange the bacon-wrapped scallops on the baking sheet and brush both sides with glaze mixture. Broil, turning once, until scallops are opaque and bacon is crispy, 3-4 minutes per side.

*Glaze may be used at once or refrigerated, covered, for up to 3 days.*
**Bacon-wrapped scallops may be cooked immediately, or refrigerated, covered, for up to 6 hours.*

# ALE CARAMELIZED ONION
# *and* BACON DIP

**MAKES 8 SERVINGS**

2 large onions

2 tablespoons olive oil

3/4 cup amber ale

2 cloves garlic, minced

8 ounces cream cheese, softened

1 cup sour cream

4 strips thick-cut bacon, cooked
and crumbled

Salt and pepper, to taste

2 green onions, chopped

Pita or bagel chips

Quarter the onions, and cut each quarter into 1/4-inch slices. Heat the oil in a large frying pan over medium heat. Add the onions and cook, stirring frequently, until transparent, about 6 minutes. Lower the heat to medium-low, cover and cook, stirring occasionally, until onions are light brown and starting to caramelize, 25–30 minutes.

Remove the lid and add the ale. Increase heat to medium and cook, stirring frequently, until most of the liquid cooks off and onions are deep golden brown. Add the garlic and cook for 1 minute. Remove from heat.

In a medium bowl, combine the cream cheese and sour cream; stir until blended. Add the caramelized onions and bacon and stir until well-combined. Season with salt and pepper and garnish with green onions. Serve with pita or bagel chips.

# CREAMY HOT BLACK BEAN DIP

**MAKES 4 SERVINGS**

1 tablespoon olive oil

2 tablespoons chopped onions

1 (4-ounce) can diced green chiles

1 tomato, diced

1 teaspoon chili powder

1/2 teaspoon salt

1 (15-ounce) can black beans with jalapeños

1 cup grated cheddar cheese

1/2 cup grated Monterey Jack cheese

4 ounces cream cheese, diced

Baked flour tortilla chips or corn chips

Heat the oil in a frying pan over medium heat and sauté the onions until tender, about 5 minutes. Add the chiles, tomato, chili powder, and salt, and cook for 5 minutes, stirring occasionally.

Spoon half of the beans with some of the liquid from the can into the bowl of a food processor, and process until smooth. Scrape down the sides and process again. Add the puréed bean mixture and remaining beans to the onion mixture and cook until hot. Add the cheddar and Monterey Jack cheeses and cream cheese. Cook, stirring constantly, until hot and bubbling. Transfer to a serving dish and serve hot with tortilla or corn chips.

# BLACK BEAN SALSA

**MAKES 8 SERVINGS**

2 medium ripe avocados, peeled and diced

2 tablespoons lime juice

1 (15-ounce) can black beans, drained and rinsed

1 (15-ounce) can whole kernel corn, drained

1 medium red bell pepper, chopped

2 green onions, chopped

2 tablespoons minced fresh cilantro

3 cloves garlic, minced

2 tablespoons olive oil

1 teaspoon red wine vinegar

1/2 teaspoon salt

1/4 teaspoon pepper

Tortilla chips

In a medium bowl, combine the avocados and lime juice; let stand, stirring gently several times, for 10 minutes.

In a large bowl, combine the beans, corn, red pepper, green onions, cilantro, and garlic.

In a small bowl, whisk together the oil, vinegar, salt, and pepper. Drizzle over bean mixture; toss to coat. Gently fold in the avocado mixture. Cover and refrigerate for at least 2 hours, or until chilled. Serve with tortilla chips.

# BACON-WRAPPED BEER BRATS

**MAKES 8 SERVING**

4 bratwurst sausages

1 (12-ounce) can or bottle regular or nonalcoholic beer

6 tablespoons brown sugar

1/2 teaspoon pepper

1/4 teaspoon cayenne pepper

8 strips bacon, cut in half

Poke bratwurst several times with a small fork, and arrange in a medium frying pan over high heat. Pour the beer around the bratwurst and bring to a boil. Reduce heat to low, cover, and simmer for 15 minutes. Remove the bratwurst from the beer, and drain on paper towels. Discard the beer.

Preheat oven to 425 degrees. Line a baking sheet with aluminum foil, place a wire rack on top, and set aside.

In a medium bowl, combine the sugar, pepper, and cayenne; set aside.

Cut each bratwurst into 4 pieces and wrap each piece with 1 half strip of bacon; secure with a toothpick. Toss the bacon-wrapped bratwurst in the sugar mixture to coat, and arrange on the wire rack. Bake, turning once, until the bacon is brown and crisp, 25–35 minutes.

# BEAN AND BEEF TAQUITOS

MAKES 12 TAQUITOS

1/2 pound ground beef

1 onion, chopped

1 jalapeño, seeded and minced

2 cloves garlic, minced

1 teaspoon ground cumin

1 teaspoon chili powder

1 cup canned refried beans

1 (8-ounce) can tomato sauce

1/4 cup water

2 tablespoons minced fresh cilantro

1/2 teaspoon salt, plus extra for sprinkling

1/2 teaspoon pepper

12 (6-inch) corn tortillas, warmed

1 egg, lightly beaten

1/2 cup vegetable oil

Salsa, sour cream, and guacamole

Preheat oven to 425 degrees. Line a large baking sheet with parchment paper.

In a large frying pan over medium-high heat, cook and break up the beef until no longer pink, about 5 minutes. Spoon beef onto paper towels to drain. Pour out all but 1 tablespoon of pan drippings, and cook the onions over medium heat until lightly browned, about 5 minutes. Add the jalapeño, garlic, cumin, and chili powder and cook until fragrant, about 2 minutes. Add refried beans, tomato sauce, water, cilantro, 1/2 teaspoon salt, and pepper. Stir in beef and cook, stirring occasionally, until mixture thickens, about 10 minutes.

Brush the top edges of a tortilla with egg. Spoon about 3 tablespoons of filling on the lower half of the tortilla; roll tightly starting at the bottom and place seam-side-down on the baking sheet. Repeat with remaining tortillas and filling. Lightly brush each rolled tortilla with oil and sprinkle with salt. Bake 15–18 minutes, turning once, until crisp and golden brown. Serve with salsa, sour cream, and guacamole.

# BEER BATTERED JALAPEÑO CHIPS

**MAKES 8 SERVINGS**

1 cup flour

1 teaspoon salt

1/2 teaspoon chili powder

1/2 teaspoon ground cumin

1/4 teaspoon garlic powder

1/4 teaspoon pepper

1 cup lager beer

Peanut oil, for frying

12 large jalapeños, seeds removed, cut in 1/3-inch slices

Salt, to taste

1 cup ranch dressing

In a medium bowl, whisk together the flour, salt, chili powder, cumin, garlic powder, and pepper. Add the beer and whisk just until smooth. Cover with plastic wrap and let rest at room temperature for 1 hour.

In a deep fryer or heavy saucepan, heat 2 inches of oil to 375 degrees. Working in batches, dip the jalapeño slices in the beet batter to coat; fry, turning once, until golden brown, 2–3 minutes. Transfer to paper towels to drain, and sprinkle with salt. Serve with ranch dressing.

# BACON CHEESE FRIES

MAKES 8 SERVINGS

1 (32-ounce) package frozen regular or crinkle-cut French-fried potatoes

Salt and pepper, to taste

1 cup grated cheddar cheese

4 green onions, thinly sliced

8 strips bacon, cooked and crumbled

1 cup ranch salad dressing

Cook fries according to package directions and sprinkle with salt and pepper.

Preheat oven broiler. Line a baking sheet with aluminum foil and spray with nonstick cooking spray.

Spread the fries evenly on the pan and sprinkle with cheese, onions, and bacon. Place in oven and broil until cheese is melted, 1–2 minutes. Serve with ranch dressing.

# SOFT BEER PRETZELS

**MAKES 8 LARGE PRETZELS**

1 (12-ounce) bottle amber ale

1 (1/4-ounce) package active dry yeast

2 tablespoons butter, melted

2 tablespoons sugar

1 1/2 teaspoons salt

4 to 4 1/2 cups flour, divided

10 cups plus 1 tablespoon water, divided

2/3 cup baking soda

1 egg yolk

Coarse salt

1 recipe Bacon Beer Cheese Dip (page 16)

In a small saucepan over medium low, heat beer to 110 degrees; remove from heat. Stir in yeast until dissolved. In a large bowl, combine butter, sugar, salt, beer mixture, and 3 cups flour; beat until smooth. Stir in just enough remaining flour to form a soft dough. Knead on a floured surface until smooth and elastic, 6–8 minutes. Place in a greased bowl, turn once, cover with plastic wrap, and let rise in a warm place until double in size, about 1 hour.

Preheat oven to 425 degrees. Prepare a baking sheet with nonstick cooking spray. Punch dough down and turn onto a lightly floured surface; divide and shape into 8 balls. Roll each ball in a 24-inch long rope and form in a pretzel shape, pinching ends to seal.

In a large stockpot, bring 10 cups water and baking soda to a boil. Drop pretzels, 2 at a time, into boiling water; cook 30 seconds. Remove and drain on paper towels. Place pretzels 2 inches apart on baking sheet.

In a small bowl, whisk together the egg yolk and 1 tablespoon water; brush over pretzels and then sprinkle with coarse salt. Bake 10–12 minutes, or until golden brown. Remove from pan to a wire rack to cool. Serve warm with Bacon Beer Cheese Dip.

# BEER-GLAZED PEANUTS

**MAKES ABOUT 5 CUPS**

4 cups raw shelled peanuts

2 cups sugar

1 cup beer

1 teaspoon salt, divided, plus extra for sprinkling

Preheat oven to 300 degrees. Line a baking sheet with parchment paper.

In a large pot, combine the peanuts, sugar, beer, and $1/2$ teaspoon salt. Heat over medium-high heat, stirring constantly, until mixture comes to a boil. Reduce heat to medium and cook, stirring constantly, until syrup reduces by half, 15–20 minutes. Add the remaining $1/2$ teaspoon salt and stir. Remove from heat.

Spread nuts on baking sheet with a silicone spatula. Bake for 10 minutes. Remove from oven and stir to separate. Bake for another 10 minutes, or until nuts are golden brown. Sprinkle nuts lightly with salt and cool on a wire rack for 10 minutes. Separate clumps of nuts and serve. Store in an airtight container.

# CRISPY ROASTED CHICKPEAS

**MAKES 8 SERVINGS**

1 teaspoon ground cumin

1 teaspoon chili powder

1/2 teaspoon salt

1/4 teaspoon cayenne pepper or black pepper

2 (15-ounce) cans garbanzo beans, drained and rinsed

2 tablespoons olive oil

Preheat oven to 350 degrees.

Combine the cumin, chili powder, salt, and cayenne in a small bowl. Set aside.

Spread the beans over several layers of paper towels and cover with another layer, blotting until completely dry. Remove and discard any loosened skins from the beans.

Place the beans in a small bowl and drizzle the oil over top; toss to coat. Spread beans evenly over a large rimmed baking sheet and bake for 30 minutes, stirring several times during cooking. Remove from the oven, stir, and cool in the pan for 5 minutes. Return to the oven and continue baking for 15–20 minutes, or until beans are golden and crunchy. Remove from oven and sprinkle with reserved spice blend, stirring to coat evenly. Serve warm or at room temperature. Store in an airtight container.

# SOUPS
### and SANDWICHES

# BEST BEER CHEESE SOUP

**MAKES 8 SERVINGS**

4 tablespoons butter

1 small onion, chopped

1 large carrot, peeled and diced

2 stalks celery, diced

3 cloves garlic, minced

1/4 cup flour

3 cups chicken stock or broth

1 (12-ounce) can or bottle regular or nonalcoholic beer

4 ounces cream cheese, softened

8 ounces sharp cheddar cheese, grated

8 ounces Colby cheese, grated, plus extra

1 cup half-and-half

1 teaspoon Dijon mustard

1/4 teaspoon Worcestershire sauce

Salt and pepper, to taste

4 strips bacon, cooked and crumbled

In a large pot, melt the butter over medium heat. Add the onion, carrot, and celery, and cook until softened, about 8 minutes. Add the garlic and cook for 1 minute.

Sprinkle in the flour and cook, stirring constantly, until smooth and slightly thickened, about 2 minutes. Whisk in the chicken stock and beer, and bring just to a boil. Reduce heat and simmer, uncovered, stirring occasionally, 40–45 minutes. Strain through a fine mesh sieve, and reserve vegetables.

Return beer mixture back to the pot and bring to a simmer over medium-low heat. Add the cream cheese and stir until melted and smooth. Add the cheddar and Colby cheeses 1/3 cup at a time, whisking after each addition until melted. Stir in the half-and-half, mustard, and Worcestershire sauce, and heat to simmering. Stir in the reserved vegetables and season with salt and pepper. Garnish with crumbled bacon and Colby cheese.

# RED CHILI
## WITH BEANS 'N' BEER

**MAKES 12 SERVINGS**

3 tablespoons vegetable oil

3 pounds flank steak, cut in
1/2-inch cubes

1 medium onion, finely chopped

1 3/4 cups beef stock or broth

2 (15.5 ounce) cans chili beans,
undrained

1 (12-ounce) can or bottle regular
or nonalcoholic beer

1 (8-ounce) can tomato sauce

1 tablespoon tomato paste

1 teaspoon hot pepper sauce

1/4 cup chili powder

1 tablespoon ground cumin

1 teaspoon garlic powder

Salt and pepper, to taste

Grated cheese, optional

Cilantro, optional

Heat the oil in a large pot over medium heat. Add the steak and onion and cook, stirring
occasionally, until lightly browned. Add the stock and bring to a simmer. Add the beans,
beer, tomato sauce, tomato paste, pepper sauce, chili powder, cumin, and garlic powder; stir
to combine. Bring mixture to a simmer and cook for 2 hours stirring occasionally. Season
with salt and pepper and garnish with cheese and cilantro, if desired.

# NAVY BEAN, SMOKED SAUSAGE
## and BEER SOUP

**MAKES 8 TO 10 SERVINGS**

1 pound dried navy beans, rinsed and picked through for small stones

4 1/2 cups chicken stock or broth

1 (12-ounce) can or bottle regular or nonalcoholic beer

1 (15-ounce) can diced tomatoes, with liquid

1 onion, chopped

2 stalks celery, chopped

3 cloves garlic, minced

1 pound smoked sausage links, cut in 1/2-inch slices

2 tablespoons Worcestershire sauce

1 bay leaf

8 strips bacon, cooked and crumbled

Salt and pepper, to taste

Flat-leaf parsley, chopped

Combine beans, stock, beer, tomatoes, onion, celery, garlic, sausage, Worcestershire sauce, and bay leaf in a large pot; heat over medium high until mixture comes to a boil. Lower heat, cover, and simmer for 4 hours, or until beans are tender, stirring occasionally and adding water if mixture becomes too thick. Stir in bacon and cook, stirring occasionally, for 10 minutes. Season with salt and pepper; discard bay leaf. Garnish with parsley.

# LOADED BAKED POTATO SOUP

**MAKES 8 SERVINGS**

4 large russet potatoes

1 cup sour cream

½ cup butter, melted

3 cups milk

1 teaspoon salt

½ teaspoon pepper

4 green onions, thinly sliced

1 cup grated sharp cheddar cheese

8 strips bacon, cooked and crumbled

Preheat oven to 400 degrees.

Prick potatoes with a fork and bake until tender, about 1 hour. Remove from oven; cool.

When cool enough to handle, peel and cut potatoes into 1-inch pieces. Transfer to a large stockpot and mash with sour cream and butter until smooth. Add the milk, salt, and pepper and bring the soup to a simmer over medium heat.

When ready to serve, divide soup among individual serving bowls and garnish with onions, cheese, and bacon.

# BEER and BACON BEEF STEW

6 strips thick-cut bacon, diced

2 pounds beef chuck, cut in 1-inch cubes

3 cloves garlic, minced

1 medium onion, diced

1 (12-ounce) can or bottle dark beer

4 cups beef stock or broth, plus more as needed

1 tablespoon Worcestershire sauce

2 to 3 tablespoons tomato paste

1/2 teaspoon paprika

1/2 teaspoon salt

1/4 teaspoon pepper

3 carrots, peeled and cut in 1/4-inch slices

1 large turnip, peeled and diced

2 tablespoons flour

Flat-leaf parsley, chopped

In a large pot, cook the bacon over medium-high heat until crisp. Transfer bacon to paper towels to drain; set aside. Add the beef to the drippings and cook until browned on all sides, 6–8 minutes. Remove beef from pot and drain on paper towels.

Drain all but 1 tablespoon of the pan drippings. Add the garlic and onion and cook until softened, about 3 minutes. Add the beer, stock, Worcestershire sauce, tomato paste, paprika, salt, and pepper and cook, stirring occasionally, for 10 minutes. Add the bacon and beef, cover, and simmer on low heat until the beef is very tender, 1 1/2–2 hours. If the liquid level gets too low, add additional stock as needed.

Add the carrots and turnip and continue to simmer, uncovered, until the vegetables are tender and the liquid is reduced, about 30 minutes.

Remove 1 cup of cooking liquid from the pan and stir in the flour until smooth. Add the flour mixture back into the pot and stir. Simmer until the stew is thick, about 10 minutes. Garnish with parsley.

# CORN, JACK, BACON and BEER CHOWDER

**MAKES 8 SERVINGS**

6 strips bacon, diced

1 large onion, chopped

4 cups corn

3 cups chicken stock or broth

1/2 cup light-bodied regular or nonalcoholic beer

1 teaspoon salt

1/4 teaspoon pepper

1 cup grated Monterey Jack cheese

1 cup heavy cream

Dash hot pepper sauce

In a large pot, cook the bacon over medium-high heat until crisp. Transfer bacon to paper towels to drain; set aside. Add the onion to the drippings and cook, stirring often, until translucent, about 4 minutes. Add the corn and cook 4 minutes more, stirring occasionally. Add the stock, beer, salt, and pepper and heat until almost boiling. Reduce heat to low and simmer for 15 minutes.

Ladle half of the soup into a food processor or blender and purée. Return blended mixture to the pot over low heat. Add the cheese a little at a time, stirring after each addition until completely melted. Slowly pour in the cream. Heat for a few more minutes, add the pepper sauce, and taste to adjust seasoning. Ladle soup into bowls and sprinkle bacon over top, to serve.

# SLOW COOKER
# BRATWURST-CHEDDAR-BEER SOUP

1 medium yellow onion, finely diced

4 large carrots, peeled and finely diced

4 cups beef stock or broth

2 cloves garlic, minced

1 tablespoon Dijon mustard

1 (12-ounce) can or bottle regular or nonalcoholic beer

2 (14-ounce) packages pre-cooked bratwursts, cut in 1/4-inch slices

2 pounds processed American cheese, cut in 1/2-inch cubes

1/2 pound finely grated sharp cheddar cheese

1 1/2 cups croutons

5 strips bacon, cooked and crumbled

In a 6-quart slow cooker, combine the onion, carrots, stock, garlic, mustard, beer, and bratwurst. Cover and cook on low for 6 hours.

Add American cheese, cover, and cook an additional hour until the cheese is fully melted. Add the cheddar cheese and stir until melted. Serve garnished with croutons and bacon.

# BACON MINESTRONE

MAKES 6 TO 8 SERVINGS

1/4 pound bacon, diced

4 cloves garlic, minced

2 carrots, peeled, cut in 1/4-inch dice

1 onion, peeled cut in 1/4-inch dice

1 leek (white part and 1 inch of green), rinsed, quartered lengthwise, cut into 1/4-inch slices

3 cups finely shredded green cabbage

1 small zucchini, quartered lengthwise, cut into 1/4-inch slices

1 potato, peeled, cut in 1/4-inch dice

4 cups chicken stock or broth

2 cups beef stock or broth

2 tablespoons tomato paste

5 tablespoons chopped fresh flat-leaf parsley, divided

2 teaspoons dried oregano

1 1/2 teaspoons dried basil

1 teaspoon black pepper

Salt, to taste

1 (15-ounce) can cannellini beans, drained and rinsed

1 (15-ounce) can kidney beans, drained and rinsed

4 ripe plum tomatoes, cut in 1/4-inch dice

1/2 cup small pasta shells

Freshly grated Parmesan cheese

Cook the bacon in a large heavy pot over medium heat until it barely starts to brown, about 5 minutes. Transfer bacon to paper towels to drain; set aside. Add the garlic, carrots, onion, and leek to the pan drippings and cook, stirring occasionally, until vegetables are tender, 8–10 minutes. Add the cabbage, zucchini, potato, chicken and beef stock, and tomato paste. Bring to a boil. Reduce heat and add 2 tablespoons parsley, oregano, basil, pepper, and salt. Simmer over medium heat for 15 minutes.

Add the cannellini and kidney beans, tomatoes, and pasta; stir and simmer until the pasta is tender, about 10 minutes. Adjust the seasonings. Stir in remaining 3 tablespoons parsley just before serving. Garnish each bowl with a generous sprinkling of cheese.

# TEX-MEX WHITE CHILI

**MAKES 6 SERVINGS**

1 tablespoon vegetable oil

1 pound lean pork tenderloin, cut in 1/2-inch cubes

Salt and pepper, to taste

1/2 cup chopped onion

2 cloves garlic, minced

3 cups chicken stock or broth

1/2 cup regular or nonalcoholic beer

1 (15-ounce) can navy beans, great Northern beans, or white kidney beans, drained and rinsed

1 (4-ounce) can diced green chiles

1 tablespoon chili powder

1/2 teaspoon ground cumin

1/2 cup grated Monterey Jack cheese

1 to 2 tablespoons snipped fresh cilantro

Heat oil in a large frying pan over medium-high heat. Add the pork and season with salt and pepper; cook until browned, stirring frequently, about 6 minutes. Transfer meat to paper towels to drain; set aside.

Add onion to same pan and cook over medium heat for 4–5 minutes, or until translucent. Add garlic and cook for another 2 minutes, or until lightly browned.

Transfer the onion mixture and reserved meat to a large soup pot. Stir in stock, beer, beans, chiles, chili powder, and cumin; bring to a boil over medium-high heat. Reduce heat to low, cover, and simmer until pork is tender, stirring occasionally, about 1 hour. When ready to serve, ladle into bowls and top with cheese and cilantro.

# CUBAN SANDWICHES

**MAKES 4 SANDWICHES**

4 soft hoagie rolls, split

2 tablespoons butter, softened

1 tablespoon mustard

4 large dill pickles, sliced lengthwise

1 pound thinly sliced roasted pork

½ pound bacon, cooked

½ pound thinly sliced ham

½ pound Jarlsberg cheese, sliced

Spray a cast-iron frying pan, griddle, or double-sided sandwich maker with nonstick cooking spray and heat on medium.

Spread one side of each roll with butter and the other side with mustard. Layer each sandwich with pickles, pork, bacon, ham, and cheese.

Arrange sandwiches in pan, in batches if necessary, and use a heavy frying pan, bacon press, or foil-wrapped brick to flatten. Grill the sandwiches 2–3 minutes on each side, or until cheese is melted and bread is golden. (If using a double-sided sandwich maker, grill for 3–4 minutes.) Cut in half diagonally and serve.

# KENTUCKY HOT BROWNS

**MAKES 6 SANDWICHES**

6 French baguette rolls

12 strips thick-cut bacon, cooked

1 ½ pounds sliced smoked
deli turkey

2 cups prepared brown gravy

1 ½ cups grated cheddar cheese

Preheat broiler.

Using a serrated knife, cut each roll lengthwise without cutting all the way through. Gently spread rolls open and arrange on a baking sheet. Toast under the broiler until lightly golden.

Remove from oven and top each roll with 2 pieces bacon and $1/6$ of the smoked turkey. Drizzle each with $1/3$ cup gravy and sprinkle with $1/4$ cup cheese. Return to the broiler and cook just until cheese melts. Transfer to individual plates and serve open-faced.

# BACON PASTRAMI REUBENS

**MAKES 4 SANDWICHES**

8 slices marble rye bread

4 tablespoons Thousand Island salad dressing, divided

8 slices Swiss cheese

½ pound thinly sliced pastrami

1 cup crisp refrigerated sauerkraut, drained, divided

8 strips thick-cut bacon, cooked and cut in half

¼ cup butter, softened

1 ½ teaspoons vegetable oil

Spread each slice of bread with $1/2$ tablespoon of dressing. Layer 4 bread slices with 1 cheese slice, $1/4$ of the pastrami, $1/4$ cup sauerkraut, 2 strips bacon, and 1 more slice of cheese. Top with remaining bread slices, dressing side down, and spread butter on the outsides of each sandwich.

Brush a large frying pan with oil and heat to medium high. Grill the sandwiches until golden brown, 2–3 minutes on each side, or until cheese is melted and bread is crispy.

# BACON-WRAPPED CHEESE DOGS

**MAKES 8 SANDWICHES**

8 strips bacon

1 small onion, sliced

8 hot dogs

4 slices American cheese

8 hot dog buns, toasted

In a large frying pan over medium heat, fry the bacon until lightly browned but still flexible. Transfer bacon to paper towels to drain, and discard all but 1 tablespoon of pan drippings. Return pan to heat and cook the onion, stirring often, until lightly browned, 5–6 minutes; remove from heat and set aside.

Preheat oven to 450 degrees. Slice each hot dog lengthwise down the middle almost, but not all the way through. Cut the cheese slices in fourths and fill the pocket of each hot dog with 2 pieces of cheese.

Wrap each hot dog with a bacon strip, securing with toothpicks if necessary. Place hot dogs on a baking sheet and bake until cheese is melted and bacon and hot dogs are hot, about 10 minutes. Serve the dogs on toasted buns topped with the onions.

# GRILLED BACON, TURKEY and JACK CHEESE

**MAKES 4 SANDWICHES**

4 tablespoons butter, softened, divided

1 medium onion, sliced

4 tablespoons barbecue sauce

8 slices sourdough bread

8 slices Monterey Jack cheese

8 strips bacon, cooked and halved

8 slices cooked turkey

8 sandwich-style pickle slices, cut in half widthwise

In a large frying pan, melt 1 tablespoon butter over medium heat; add the onion and cook, stirring frequently until tender, about 5 minutes. Remove cooked onion to a separate dish and set aside. Do not wipe out pan.

Spread barbecue sauce on 4 slices of bread. Top each with 1 slice of cheese, 4 half strips of bacon, 2 turkey slices, and 2 pickle slices. Divide the onions among the sandwiches and top each with remaining cheese slices. Cover with remaining slices of bread.

Heat the frying pan over medium-low heat and melt the remaining 3 tablespoons butter. Cook sandwiches on both sides until golden brown and cheese has melted, about 3 minutes per side.

# BACON *and* SHRIMP PO' BOYS

**MAKES 4 SANDWICHES**

2 tablespoons mayonnaise

1 tablespoon ranch salad dressing

1 ½ teaspoons mustard

1 teaspoon hot red pepper sauce

¼ teaspoon pepper

1 cup grated sharp cheddar cheese

1 ½ cups shredded iceberg lettuce

3 strips bacon, cooked and finely crumbled

4 hoagie buns, split and toasted

16 large shrimp, peeled, deveined, and cooked

2 tomatoes, each cut in 4 slices

In a medium bowl, combine the mayonnaise, dressing, mustard, hot sauce, and pepper. Add the cheese, lettuce, and bacon; toss to coat.

Divide the mixture over the bottom halves of each roll and top with 4 shrimp, and 2 tomato slices. Replace tops, cut sandwiches on the diagonal, and serve.

# BACON CRAB MELTS

**MAKES 4 SANDWICHES**

4 tablespoons mayonnaise

1 stalk celery, finely chopped

1 tablespoon lemon juice

1/2 teaspoon seafood seasoning, such as Old Bay

1/2 teaspoon Dijon mustard

1/8 teaspoon salt

1/8 teaspoon pepper

12 ounces lump crabmeat, drained and picked through for shells

4 tablespoons butter, softened

8 slices sourdough bread

8 thin slices cheddar cheese

8 strips bacon, cooked

2 Roma tomatoes, cut in 1/4-inch slices

In a medium bowl, combine the mayonnaise, celery, lemon juice, seasoning, mustard, salt, and pepper. Add the crabmeat and stir gently to combine.

Spread butter on 4 bread slices. Flip bread over and top each with 1 slice of cheese. Divide the crab mixture between the 4 bread slices and spread over the cheese. Top with bacon strips, tomatoes, remaining cheese slices, and remaining 4 bread slices. Spread remaining butter on top of sandwiches.

Heat a large frying pan over medium heat and cook the sandwiches, until both sides are golden brown and cheese has melted, about 3 minutes per side.

# SLOW COOKER BACON BARBECUE CHICKEN ROLLS

**MAKES 8 SANDWICHES**

4 boneless, skinless chicken breasts (about 1 ½ pounds)

2 cups barbecue sauce

8 large onion rolls, split

3 tablespoons butter, melted

16 strips bacon, cooked and halved

2 cups grated cheddar cheese

Place chicken breasts in a 3- to 4-quart slow cooker and pour barbecue sauce over top. Cook on low setting until chicken is tender and cooked through, 6–7 hours. Remove chicken to a cutting board and cool for 15 minutes. Shred chicken with 2 forks and return to slow cooker.

Preheat oven to 425 degrees.

Cover a baking sheet with aluminum foil and arrange roll tops and bottoms cut-side up on top of the foil; brush with the butter. Bake until edges are lightly browned, about 5 minutes. Transfer roll tops to a cooling rack.

Using a slotted spoon, top each roll bottom with a generous spoonful of shredded chicken. Layer each with 4 halves of bacon, and sprinkle with cheese. Return to oven and bake until cheese is melted, 3–4 minutes. Replace roll tops and serve.

# EASY MEALS

# BEER BACON MAC and CHEESE

MAKES 8 TO 10 SERVINGS

1 (16-ounce) package elbow macaroni

1/4 cup butter

2 cloves garlic, minced

3 tablespoons flour

2 teaspoons dry mustard

1 teaspoon salt

3/4 teaspoon pepper

2 1/2 cups milk

3/4 cup regular or nonalcoholic light beer

1/4 cup heavy cream

3 cups grated cheddar cheese, divided

2 cups grated Gruyère cheese

2 tablespoons grated Parmesan cheese, divided

2 green onions, minced

6 strips bacon, cooked and crumbled

Preheat oven to 400 degrees. Prepare a 3-quart baking dish with nonstick cooking spray. Cook macaroni according to package directions; drain and set aside.

In a large saucepan, melt the butter over medium heat. Add the garlic, and cook, stirring for 1 minute. Stir in the flour, mustard, salt, and pepper until smooth. Gradually whisk in the milk, beer, and cream and bring to a boil; cook and stir for 2 minutes, or until thickened. Reduce heat and stir in 2 cups of cheddar, the Gruyère, and 1 tablespoon Parmesan until melted. Add the onions.

Stir macaroni into sauce and transfer to baking dish. Sprinkle remaining cheddar and Parmesan cheese evenly over top. Bake, uncovered, for 15–20 minutes, or until golden brown and heated through. Top with bacon and let stand for 5 minutes before serving.

# BEER BARBECUE SLOW COOKER RIBS

**MAKES 4 TO 6 SERVINGS**

3 pounds bone-in pork spareribs, cut in individual ribs

3 tablespoons liquid smoke flavoring

2 tablespoons packed dark brown sugar

1 tablespoon chili powder

2 teaspoons paprika

1 teaspoon garlic powder

1/2 teaspoon salt

1/2 teaspoon pepper

1 (12-ounce) can or bottle regular or nonalcoholic beer

2 cups barbecue sauce

Trim any excess fat away from the ribs and remove the membrane. Arrange ribs on a baking sheet and brush all sides with the liquid smoke.

In a small bowl, combine the sugar, chili powder, paprika, garlic powder, salt, and pepper. Rub the mixture all over the ribs. Pour the beer in a 6-quart slow cooker and arrange the ribs inside. Cover and cook on low for 6 hours. Remove ribs from the slow cooker and allow them to rest for 10 minutes.

Preheat the grill to medium-high heat and lightly oil the grill grate. Brush ribs with barbecue sauce and place on the grill, turning once, until lightly browned, 6–8 minutes. Transfer to a serving platter and brush with more barbecue sauce.

# ORANGE MOLASSES STOUT CHICKEN

**MAKES 4 TO 6 SERVINGS**

1 (12-ounce) can or bottle stout beer, such as Guinness

1/4 cup olive oil

1/4 cup molasses

1/4 cup orange marmalade

2 teaspoons Dijon mustard

2 cloves garlic, minced

1 teaspoon salt

1/2 teaspoon pepper

1 (3 to 4-pound) whole chicken, cut into pieces*

In a medium bowl, whisk together the beer, oil, molasses, marmalade, mustard, garlic, salt, and pepper. Place the chicken pieces in a large ziplock bag along with the marinade. Seal tightly, toss to coat, and refrigerate for at least 4 hours or overnight, turning occasionally.

Remove chicken from the bag and pour the marinade into a medium saucepan. Bring to a boil over medium-high heat for 2 minutes. Remove from heat and cool. Pour 1 cup of the marinade in a small dish for basting; reserve the remainder.

Preheat the grill for indirect cooking over medium heat (350–450 degrees) and lightly oil the grill grate. Cook the chicken pieces skin side up with the lid closed until the juices run clear and the meat is no longer pink at the bone, 30–40 minutes for wings, and 40–50 minutes for breasts, drumsticks, and thighs. Baste with the marinade during the last 10 minutes of grilling time, turning the pieces once. Remove chicken to a serving platter and serve with the reserved marinade.

*If you prefer, ask your butcher or grocer's meat department to cut up the chicken for you, or you can use 3 to 4 pounds of your favorite chicken pieces.*

# BACON RIB-EYE STEAKS
## WITH BACON CHIVE BUTTER

MAKES 4 SERVINGS

### Bacon Chive Butter

4 tablespoons butter, softened

1 tablespoon chopped fresh chives

1 strip bacon, cooked and finely crumbled

1 small clove garlic, minced

### Steaks

¼ cup soy sauce

2 tablespoons olive oil

2 tablespoons ketchup

¼ teaspoon dry mustard

1 clove garlic, minced

4 (8 to 10-ounce) rib-eye steaks, cut 1-inch thick

Pepper, to taste

8 strips bacon, partially cooked

### Bacon Chive Butter

Combine the butter, chives, bacon, and garlic together in a small bowl until mixed well. Place mixture on a piece of plastic wrap and roll into a log. Twist ends of plastic wrap and chill in refrigerator for at least 4 hours.

### Steaks

In a shallow dish or large ziplock bag, combine the soy sauce, oil, ketchup, mustard, and garlic. Add the meat and turn or toss to coat. Marinate in the refrigerator for 4 hours, turning several times.

Preheat grill to medium-high heat.

Remove steaks from marinade and season with pepper. Discard the marinade. Wrap the edges of each steak with 2 strips of bacon, securing ends with toothpicks. Grill steaks to desired doneness, turning once halfway through grilling. Remove butter from refrigerator and slice into 4 pieces, topping each hot steak with a pat of butter.

# BACON, CHICKEN, CHEDDAR and BBQ PIZZA

**MAKES 4 SERVINGS**

⅓ to ½ cup barbecue sauce

1 (12-inch-round) prebaked Italian pizza crust

¾ cup chopped cooked chicken breast

8 strips bacon, cooked and crumbled

1 ¼ cups grated cheddar cheese

¼ cup finely sliced red onion, optional

Chopped fresh flat-leaf parsley, optional

Preheat oven to 425 degrees.

Spread the barbecue sauce on the pizza crust and sprinkle evenly with the chicken, bacon, cheese, and onion, if using.

Bake for 8–10 minutes, or until cheese is bubbly. Remove from the oven, garnish with parsley, if desired, cut into 8 slices, and serve.

# BACON CHEESEBURGER MEATLOAF

**MAKES 6 TO 8 SERVINGS**

8 strips bacon

1 small onion, finely chopped

1 ½ pounds lean ground beef

1 egg, lightly beaten

¼ cup evaporated milk

½ teaspoon salt

¼ teaspoon pepper

8 ounces Colby cheese, grated and divided

½ cup seasoned breadcrumbs

Preheat oven to 350 degrees.

In a frying pan, cook bacon over medium heat until crisp. Remove and drain on paper towels; crumble, and set aside. Discard all but 1 tablespoon of the pan drippings. Add the onion to the pan and cook until soft; remove from heat.

In a large bowl, mix together the beef, egg, milk, salt, and pepper. Add the onion, 2/3 of the cheese, and all but 1 tablespoon of bacon. Stir in breadcrumbs and mix until combined. Shape into a loaf and transfer to a shallow baking dish. Bake for 1 hour.

Remove from oven, drain fat, and sprinkle with remaining cheese and bacon. Return to oven and bake until cheese is melted, about 5 minutes more.

# MAPLE BACON DRUMSTICKS

**MAKES 4 SERVINGS**

8 chicken drumsticks

½ teaspoon pepper

8 strips bacon

¼ cup maple syrup

1 ½ teaspoons Worcestershire sauce

¼ cup ketchup

2 cloves garlic, minced

Preheat oven to 375 degrees. Prepare a 9 x 13-inch baking dish liberally with nonstick cooking spray.

Sprinkle the drumsticks evenly with pepper. Wrap 1 strip of bacon tightly around each drumstick, securing ends with toothpicks.

Combine the syrup, Worcestershire sauce, ketchup, and garlic in a small bowl and brush over the drumsticks, coating all sides. Arrange in baking dish and bake for 50–60 minutes, or until the thickest part of the chicken registers 160 degrees on a meat thermometer, turning once during bake time.

# BAKED SALMON WITH BACON

**MAKES 4 SERVINGS**

1 tablespoon butter

1 large shallot, finely chopped

8 strips bacon, diced

1 tablespoon chopped fresh dill

2 tablespoons lemon juice

4 (6-ounce) wild salmon fillets

Preheat oven to 400 degrees.

Cut a piece of aluminum foil double the size of a 9 x 13-inch baking dish and fit one half of it into the bottom of the dish; spray with nonstick cooking spray.

Over medium heat, melt the butter in a large sauté pan and cook the shallot until softened. Add the bacon and cook until light golden brown. Add the dill and lemon juice and cook for 1 minute; remove from heat.

Arrange the salmon on the foil in the baking dish and spoon the bacon mixture over top. Fold the other half of the foil over the fish and crimp the edges to make a packet. Bake for about 20 minutes, or until salmon is opaque and flakes easily with a fork.

# CREOLE RED BEANS AND RICE

**MAKES 6 SERVINGS**

4 slices bacon

1/2 pound andouille sausage, cut in 1/2-inch slices

1 cup chopped ham

2 onions, chopped

1 green bell pepper, seeded and chopped

4 stalks celery, chopped

2 cloves garlic, minced

1 bay leaf

1 teaspoon dried thyme

1/2 teaspoon salt

1/2 teaspoon pepper

4 cups chicken stock or broth

2 (15-ounce) cans kidney beans, drained and rinsed

3 Roma tomatoes, chopped

1 tablespoon red wine or balsamic vinegar

1 teaspoon hot pepper sauce

1 smoked ham hock

4 cups hot, cooked white rice

In a large heavy pot, cook the bacon over medium-high heat until it just starts to brown. Add the sausage and ham and continue cooking, stirring, until sausage is browned. Add the onions, pepper, celery, garlic, bay leaf, thyme, salt, and pepper, and continue cooking, stirring occasionally, until vegetables are tender.

Add the stock, beans, tomatoes, vinegar, hot sauce, and ham hock. Continue cooking and stirring for 5 minutes. Increase the heat to high and bring the mixture to a boil. Reduce heat to medium low and simmer, uncovered, for 1 1/2 hours, to blend flavors and thicken. Add a little water if the mixture gets too thick.

Remove the ham hock and let it cool. Transfer 1/4 of the bean mixture to a food processor or blender and purée until smooth; return the mixture to the pot and stir. Remove the meat from the ham hock, cut into small pieces, and add to the pot; heat for 3 more minutes. Serve over hot rice.

# GERMAN POTATO SALAD
## WITH BEER DRESSING

**MAKES 8 SERVINGS**

2 pounds medium red potatoes

2 teaspoons salt, divided

3 thick strips bacon

1 small onion, minced

2/3 cup regular or nonalcoholic beer

1/2 cup apple cider vinegar

2 teaspoons sugar

1 tablespoon stone-ground mustard

2 tablespoons vegetable oil

1/4 teaspoon pepper

1/4 cup thinly sliced green onions

1/4 cup minced fresh Italian parsley

Place the potatoes in a large saucepan and cover with cold water. Bring to a boil over medium-high heat. Add 1 teaspoon of salt, reduce heat to medium, and cook 20–30 minutes, or until potatoes are tender. Drain and cool for 30 minutes.

Cook the bacon in a large frying pan over medium heat until crispy; remove bacon to a paper towel to drain. Add the onion to the pan drippings and sauté over medium heat until tender, about 3 minutes. Add the beer, vinegar, and sugar; stir. Increase heat to medium high and bring to a boil. Cook until the liquid is slightly reduced, about 5 minutes. Whisk in the mustard, oil, remaining 1 teaspoon salt, and pepper.

Peel the cooled potatoes, cut in 1/4-inch slices, and arrange in a large serving bowl. Drizzle with the hot dressing and gently toss to combine. Let sit at room temperature for at least 30 minutes to allow the potatoes to absorb some of the dressing. Crumble the bacon and add to the potatoes along with the green onions and parsley. Stir gently and serve.

# BACON *and* CHICKEN RANCH SALAD

**MAKES 6 SERVINGS**

8 strips bacon, chopped

1 pound boneless, skinless chicken breasts, cut in 1-inch pieces

½ teaspoon paprika

¼ teaspoon salt

¼ teaspoon pepper

¼ teaspoon garlic powder

1 pound fresh baby spinach, washed and stems removed

2 cups halved grape tomatoes

¼ red onion, sliced

1 cup grated mild cheddar cheese

1 large English cucumber, sliced

1 cup ranch salad dressing

Cook the bacon in a large frying pan over medium heat until browned and crispy. Transfer bacon to paper towels to drain, and discard all but 1 tablespoon of pan drippings.

Return pan to heat, add the chicken and cook, stirring occasionally, until chicken is cooked through and lightly browned, about 10 minutes. Sprinkle with paprika, salt, pepper, and garlic powder, and stir to coat. Remove from heat, cover, and set aside.

In a large bowl, combine the spinach, tomatoes, onion, cheese, and cucumber. Drizzle with the dressing and toss gently. Divide the salad evenly among 6 chilled salad plates and top with the warm chicken. Sprinkle reserved bacon on top and serve.

# SKILLET BACON
## and BEER GREEN BEANS

**MAKES 6 SERVINGS**

⅓ pound sliced bacon, diced

½ cup beer

4 tablespoons butter

1 pound fresh green beans, trimmed and cut in 2-inch pieces

3 tablespoons brown sugar

3 tablespoons white vinegar

4 teaspoons cornstarch

2 teaspoons grated onion

Salt and pepper, to taste

In a large frying pan over medium heat, cook bacon until crisp. Remove bacon from pan and drain on paper towels; set aside.

In a large saucepan over medium heat, combine the beer and butter and heat until mixture just starts to boil. Add the beans and stir. Reduce heat, cover, and simmer until beans are crisp-tender, about 5 minutes. Remove beans from the cooking liquid to a dish, cover, and keep warm.

Add the sugar, vinegar, cornstarch, and onion to the cooking liquid and whisk to combine. Cook over medium heat until mixture boils. Continue cooking, whisking constantly, until thickened, 1–2 minutes. Return beans to the pan and stir to coat. Season with salt and pepper. Transfer to a serving dish and top with reserved bacon.

# BACON MACARONI SALAD

1 pound uncooked elbow macaroni

1 large tomato, chopped

2 stalks celery, chopped

3 green onions, finely chopped

1 cup mayonnaise

¼ cup ranch dressing

1 tablespoon balsamic vinegar

¼ teaspoon salt

¼ teaspoon pepper

1 cup grated sharp cheddar cheese

1 pound bacon, cooked and crumbled

Cook macaroni according to package directions; drain and rinse in cold water. Transfer to a large bowl; stir in tomato, celery, and onions.

In a small bowl, whisk together the mayonnaise, dressing, vinegar, salt, and pepper. Pour over macaroni and toss to coat. Refrigerate, covered, for at least 2 hours or overnight. Just before serving, mix in cheese and bacon.

# BEST TACO SALAD

1 pound lean ground beef

1 (1.25-ounce) package taco seasoning mix

1 (15-ounce) can kidney beans, drained and rinsed

1/4 cup water

2 ripe tomatoes, diced

2 cups grated Mexican blend cheese

4 green onions, chopped

1 head iceberg lettuce, chopped

1 cup Catalina, ranch, or Italian salad dressing

1 (13-ounce) bag plain or taco-flavored tortilla chips

1 cup salsa

1 cup sour cream

In a large frying pan, crumble and brown the beef over medium-high heat until no longer pink. Drain the grease and add the seasoning mix, beans, and water. Cook over medium heat, stirring, until slightly thickened, about 5 minutes. Remove from heat and cool to room temperature. Transfer to a covered container and refrigerate for at least 2 hours.

In a large serving bowl, combine the beef mixture, tomatoes, cheese, onions, and lettuce. Add the dressing and mix well. Crumble the tortilla chips into bite-size pieces, add to the salad, and toss to evenly distribute. Serve with salsa and sour cream.

# LAYERED POTLUCK SALAD

**MAKES 8 SERVINGS**

1 head romaine lettuce, chopped

1/2 cup chopped celery

1 (8-ounce) can sliced water chestnuts, drained and chopped

2 cups grated cheddar cheese

1 bunch green onions, chopped

1 (15-ounce) can garbanzo beans, drained and rinsed

1 (16-ounce) package frozen green peas, partially thawed

1 cup mayonnaise

1/2 cup sour cream

1 teaspoon sugar

1/2 teaspoon seasoning salt

1/4 teaspoon garlic powder

1/4 teaspoon pepper

1/2 pound bacon, cooked and crumbled

4 hard-boiled eggs, peeled and chopped

1 large tomato, chopped and drained

In a clear glass serving or trifle bowl, layer the lettuce, celery, water chestnuts, cheese, onions, beans, and peas.

In a medium bowl, combine the mayonnaise, sour cream, sugar, seasoning salt, garlic powder, and pepper; stir until smooth. Spread evenly over the salad to the edge of the bowl. Cover and refrigerate overnight.

When ready to serve, remove the salad from the refrigerator and top with the bacon, eggs, and tomato; toss to incorporate the dressing.

# BACON, CHEDDAR
## and BEER POTATOES

1/4 cup butter

1/4 cup flour

1 teaspoon garlic powder

1/4 teaspoon cayenne pepper

1/2 teaspoon paprika

1 teaspoon salt

1/2 teaspoon pepper

1/2 cup wheat beer

1/2 cup chicken stock or broth

3/4 cup half-and-half

1 cup milk

1 teaspoon Worcestershire sauce

8 ounces mild cheddar cheese, grated

3 pounds red potatoes, cut in 1/4-inch slices

1 pound bacon, cooked, and crumbled

Preheat oven to 350 degrees. Prepare a 3-quart casserole dish with nonstick cooking spray.

Melt butter in a saucepan over medium heat; add flour and whisk until smooth. Cook, whisking constantly, for 2 minutes. Add garlic powder, cayenne, paprika, salt, and pepper, and whisk to combine. Slowly add the beer, stock, half-and-half, milk, and Worcestershire sauce; whisk until smooth. Add the cheese, whisking constantly until cheese melts and mixture is smooth. Reduce heat to low and simmer, stirring occasionally, for 5 minutes.

Layer 1/4 of the potatoes in the casserole dish and top with 1/4 of the cheese sauce. Sprinkle with half of the bacon, reserving the rest. Repeat potato and cheese sauce layers. Cover and bake until potatoes are tender, 60–80 minutes. Uncover, sprinkle with reserved bacon and bake for 10 more minutes. Remove from oven and cool for 10 minutes before serving.

# SWEET POTATO HASH

**MAKES 6 SERVINGS**

1 ½ pounds sweet potatoes, peeled, cut in ½-inch dice

Salt, to taste

½ pound bacon, cut in 1-inch pieces

1 cup diced onion

1 cup diced red bell pepper

2 cloves garlic, minced

Pepper, to taste

Place the potatoes in a large pot, cover with 2 inches of cold water, and generously season with salt. Bring to a boil over high heat, reduce to medium, and simmer for 5 minutes, or until barely tender; drain and set aside.

Cook the bacon in a large frying pan over medium heat until crisp. Remove bacon from pan and drain on paper towels; set aside.

Discard all but 2 tablespoons of pan drippings. Add the onion and cook for 5 minutes, or until soft. Add the potatoes and cook for 8 minutes, stirring occasionally, until potatoes are lightly browned. Add the bell pepper and garlic and cook for several minutes more, stirring occasionally, until potatoes are golden brown and bell pepper is tender. Add the bacon and toss. Season with salt and pepper and serve.

# BEER, BACON *AND* CHEDDAR CORNBREAD

1 1/2 cups cornmeal

1 1/2 cups flour

2 tablespoons sugar

1 1/2 tablespoons baking powder

3/4 teaspoon salt

1 1/2 cups grated sharp cheddar cheese, divided

3 eggs

1/2 cup milk

1/3 cup sour cream

1 cup lager beer

1/2 cup butter, melted

6 strips thick-cut bacon, cooked and crumbled

Preheat oven to 375 degrees. Lightly prepare a 9 x 13-inch baking dish with nonstick cooking spray.

In a large bowl, combine the cornmeal, flour, sugar, baking powder, salt, and 1/2 cup cheese.

In a medium bowl, combine the eggs, milk, sour cream, beer, and butter; stir until well-blended. Add the egg mixture to the cornmeal mixture and stir until just combined. Add the bacon and stir to distribute evenly throughout the batter.

Spread evenly in the bottom of the baking dish and sprinkle the remaining 1 cup of cheese over the top. Bake for 30-35 minutes, or until lightly browned and a toothpick inserted into the center comes out clean. Cut in squares to serve.

# ULTIMATE BACON GARLIC MASHED POTATOES

**MAKES 8 SERVINGS**

1/4 cup butter, plus extra

4 1/2 pounds russet potatoes, peeled

1 (8-ounce) package cream cheese, room temperature

1 cup sour cream

1 clove garlic, minced

1 teaspoon salt

1/2 teaspoon pepper

2 green onions, finely chopped

8 strips bacon, cooked and crumbled

1/4 teaspoon paprika

Preheat oven to 400 degrees. Lightly butter a 2-quart casserole dish.

Place potatoes in a large pot, cover with water, and boil until fork tender. Remove from heat, drain and mash well; set aside.

In a large bowl, beat the cream cheese and sour cream together until smooth. Gradually add potatoes, garlic, salt, and pepper, beating until smooth. Stir in the onions and bacon.

Spread mixture evenly into the baking dish. Cut the 1/4 cup of butter into small cubes and dot the potatoes; sprinkle with paprika. Cover and bake until heated through, 35–45 minutes.

# BACON MUSHROOMS WITH BEER GLAZE

**MAKES 6 SERVINGS**

½ pound bacon, chopped

1 medium onion, sliced

1 pound medium-size button mushrooms, trimmed, cut in half

¼ cup regular or nonalcoholic beer, of choice

Salt and pepper, to taste

2 tablespoons chopped fresh chives

In a large frying pan, cook the bacon over medium heat until crispy. Use a slotted spoon to transfer the bacon to paper towels to drain. Pour out all but 1 tablespoon of the pan drippings, and return the pan to the stove.

Add the onion and sauté over medium heat, stirring occasionally, until tender and lightly browned, about 5 minutes. Add the mushrooms and sauté, stirring occasionally until browned, about 6 minutes.

Add the beer (mixture may foam up) and increase heat to medium high. Cook, stirring occasionally, until beer reduces by half and becomes syrupy, about 6 minutes. Stir in the reserved bacon, and sprinkle with salt, pepper, and chives; serve immediately.

# PORK LOVERS' MAPLE BAKED BEANS

2 cups dried navy beans

1 1/2 cups water, plus extra for cooking beans

1/2 cup regular or nonalcoholic beer

1/2 cup maple syrup

1 teaspoon dry mustard

1 teaspoon salt

6 strips bacon, chopped

1 onion, chopped

1 smoked ham hock

2 tablespoons butter, softened

2 tablespoons dark brown sugar

Place the beans in a large pot, add enough water to cover beans by 2 inches, and bring to a boil over high heat. Boil for 30 minutes. Drain beans and discard cooking liquid.

Preheat oven to 325 degrees.

In a medium bowl, combine 1 1/2 cups water, beer, syrup, mustard, and salt.

Place the bacon in the bottom of a Dutch oven and spoon half of the beans and half of the onion evenly over top. Add the ham hock and remaining beans and onion. Pour the syrup mixture over the beans and cover with a lid. Bake for 3 hours, or until beans are tender and the meat from the ham hock is pulling away from the bone. Add more water if necessary during baking time.

Remove from oven and remove the ham hock to a cutting board to cool. When cool enough to handle, remove the meat, chop, and stir into the beans.

In a small bowl, combine the butter and sugar. Dot the beans with butter mixture and return to the oven, uncovered, and bake for 30 minutes.

# LUCKY BLACK-EYED PEAS

6 strips bacon

1 large onion, chopped

1 stalk celery, diced

4 cloves garlic, minced

5 1/2 cups chicken stock or broth

1/2 cup regular or nonalcoholic beer

1/2 teaspoon salt

1/4 teaspoon pepper

4 cups fresh or frozen black-eyed peas

In a large pot or Dutch oven, cook bacon over medium heat until crisp; drain on paper towels and discard all but 2 tablespoons of the drippings.

Add the onion, celery, and garlic to the pot and sauté over medium heat until tender, about 5 minutes. Add the stock, beer, salt, pepper, and peas. Increase heat to medium high and bring to a boil. Crumble the bacon and add to the pot. Lower the heat, cover, and simmer until peas are tender, about 1 hour.

# GRILLED BACON-WRAPPED CORN

**MAKES 8 SERVINGS**

8 strips bacon

8 large ears sweet corn,
husks and silk removed

Freshly ground black pepper

Cut 8, 12-inch square pieces of heavy-duty aluminum foil. Spiral-wrap 1 strip of bacon around each ear of corn and place on a square of foil. Sprinkle with pepper and wrap the corn securely in the foil, twisting the ends.

Preheat grill to medium heat. Grill foil-wrapped corn, turning frequently, until corn is tender, about 15 minutes. Remove foil and return corn to grill, turning frequently, until bacon is crisp, 4–5 minutes.

# BACON *and* CHEESE HASSELBACK POTATOES

**MAKES 4 SERVINGS**

4 large Yukon gold potatoes

4 tablespoons cold butter

Salt and pepper, to taste

8 strips bacon, cut in 1-inch pieces

½ cup grated fresh Parmesan cheese

Microgreens, optional

Preheat oven to 425 degrees. Line a baking sheet with aluminum foil.

Using a sharp knife, make ¼-inch vertical cuts in each potato, without cutting all the way through the potato. Slice the butter into thin pieces and then cut in half. Place butter slices in alternating slits of each potato. Sprinkle with salt and pepper.

Place potatoes on baking sheet and bake until skin is crispy and potato is tender, 40–45 minutes.

Cook the bacon in a large frying pan over medium heat until crisp. Transfer bacon to paper towels to drain; set aside.

Remove potatoes from oven and cool on the pan for 10 minutes. Spread potatoes open and sprinkle with cheese. Evenly divide bacon into fourths and tuck the bacon pieces into the slits of each potato. Return potatoes to the oven and bake until cheese melts, about 4 more minutes. Garnish with microgreens, if desired.

# SWEET TREATS

# AMAZING CHOCOLATE CHIP COOKIE DOUGH DIP

1 (15-ounce) can garbanzo beans, drained and rinsed

1/4 cup almond or peanut butter

1/4 cup softened cream cheese

1/4 cup firmly packed brown sugar

2 tablespoons warm water

2 tablespoons maple syrup

2 tablespoons quick-cooking oats

1 tablespoon vanilla

1/4 teaspoon salt

1/8 teaspoon baking soda

1/2 cup mini chocolate chips

Fresh strawberries and graham cracker sticks, for dipping

Combine the beans, almond or peanut butter, cream cheese, sugar, water, syrup, oats, vanilla, salt, and baking soda in the bowl of a food processor. Process until batter is blended. Scrape down the sides and process again until smooth.

Transfer to a serving bowl and fold in chocolate chips. Serve with strawberries and graham cracker sticks.

# MAPLE BACON CRUNCH

**MAKES 6 SERVINGS**

1 (8-ounce) can refrigerated crescent seamless dough sheet or crescent rolls

1 pound bacon

1/2 cup maple syrup, divided

3/4 cup packed dark brown sugar, divided

Preheat oven to 325 degrees. Line a rimmed baking sheet with parchment paper and spray with nonstick cooking spray.

Place the dough sheet on baking pan; press and stretch to a thickness of 1/4 inch. If using crescent roll dough, pinch perforations together. Prick dough all over with a fork.

In a large frying pan over medium heat, cook the bacon until it is just beginning to brown but not crispy. Transfer bacon to paper towels and drain. Cut the bacon in 1-inch pieces and set aside.

Drizzle 1/4 cup of syrup over the dough and sprinkle with 1/4 cup sugar. Arrange the bacon pieces on top and drizzle with remaining syrup and sprinkle with remaining sugar.

Bake for 25 minutes, or until browned and bubbling. Remove from oven and cool in the pan to room temperature. Cut or break into pieces to serve.

# BACON BREAD PUDDING
## WITH VANILLA SAUCE

MAKES 8 SERVINGS

1 (12-count) package Hawaiian dinner rolls

2 1/2 cups whole milk, divided

1 cup heavy cream

5 eggs, divided

1/2 cup sugar

2 teaspoons vanilla, divided

1/2 teaspoon salt

1/4 teaspoon nutmeg

8 strips bacon, cooked crisp, finely crumbled

1/2 cup packed dark brown sugar

1 tablespoon flour

1/4 teaspoon cinnamon

2 tablespoons butter, melted

One day before preparing recipe, cut the rolls into 1-inch cubes and arrange on a large baking sheet. Air dry for 24 hours.

Preheat oven to 350 degrees. Prepare an 8 x 8-inch baking dish with nonstick cooking spray.

In a large bowl, combine 1 1/4 cups milk, cream, 4 eggs, sugar, 1 teaspoon vanilla, salt, and nutmeg; whisk to blend. Add bacon and stir to combine. Arrange bread cubes in baking dish and drizzle the egg mixture over top, stirring to coat bread evenly. Bake for 45 minutes, or until top is lightly browned and egg mixture is set.

In a large saucepan, combine 1 1/4 cups milk, brown sugar, flour, cinnamon, 1 egg, and butter; whisk until smooth. Heat over medium heat, whisking constantly until mixture is thickened and coats the back of a spoon, 10–12 minutes. Stir in 1 teaspoon vanilla and remove from heat. Drizzle sauce over warm bread pudding to serve.

# BEER CARAMEL CORN

**MAKES 10 SERVINGS**

10 cups popped popcorn

1 cup roughly chopped pecan halves

1 cup broken pretzel sticks, (1-inch pieces)

1 (12-ounce) bottle brown ale

3 tablespoons butter

2 cups brown sugar

1 cup heavy cream

1/4 teaspoon salt

2 teaspoons vanilla

1/2 teaspoon baking soda

Preheat oven to 250 degrees.

Spread the popcorn, pecans, and pretzels on a large rimmed baking sheet and stir to combine; set aside.

In a large saucepan over medium heat, combine the ale and butter and bring to a boil, stirring occasionally. Cook until mixture is reduced by 1/4. Add the sugar, stir to dissolve, and boil without stirring until mixture reaches 248 degrees on a candy thermometer. Slowly add the cream, stirring to incorporate. Cook for about 5 minutes until caramel is thick. Remove from heat and add the salt, vanilla, and baking soda. The mixture will foam up.

Drizzle evenly over the popcorn mixture, and mix until well coated. Bake for 1 hour, stirring every 15 minutes. Remove pan from oven and spread mixture on parchment paper. Cool to room temperature before breaking apart. Store in a tightly covered container.

# FLOURLESS CHOCOLATE CHIP BLONDIES

**MAKES 16 COOKIES**

1 (15-ounce) can garbanzo beans, drained and rinsed

1/2 cup natural peanut butter

1/3 cup maple syrup

1 egg

2 teaspoons vanilla

1/2 teaspoon salt

1/4 teaspoon baking powder

1/4 teaspoon baking soda

1/2 cup semisweet chocolate chips

Preheat oven to 350 degrees. Prepare an 8 x 8-inch baking pan with nonstick cooking spray.

Combine the beans, peanut butter, syrup, egg, vanilla, salt, baking powder, and baking soda in bowl of a food processor. Process until batter is blended. Scrape down the sides of the bowl and process again until batter is smooth.

Fold in the chocolate chips and spread the batter evenly in the baking pan. Bake for 30 minutes, or until the edges are lightly browned and a toothpick inserted into the center comes out clean. Cool on a wire rack. When ready to serve, cut into squares.

# SPICY GINGERBREAD CAKE

**MAKES 8 TO 10 SERVINGS**

1 cup stout beer, such as Guinness

1 cup molasses

1 1/2 teaspoons baking soda

3 eggs

1/2 cup sugar

1/2 cup packed dark brown sugar

3/4 cup vegetable oil

2 cups flour

2 tablespoons ground ginger

1 1/2 teaspoons baking powder

3/4 teaspoon ground cinnamon

1/4 teaspoon ground cloves

1/4 teaspoon ground nutmeg

1 tablespoon peeled and grated, fresh gingerroot

Sweetened whipped cream

Preheat oven to 350 degrees. Prepare a 12-cup Bundt pan with nonstick cooking spray and dust with flour.

In a large saucepan over high heat, combine the beer and molasses and bring to a boil, stirring gently. Remove from heat and stir in the baking soda; allow mixture to sit for 10 minutes, or until foam subsides.

In a medium bowl, whisk together the eggs, sugar, and brown sugar; whisk in the oil to blend. In a large bowl, whisk together the flour, ginger, baking powder, cinnamon, cloves, and nutmeg. Combine the beer mixture with the egg mixture until blended; whisk into the flour mixture. Add the gingerroot and stir to combine.

Pour the batter into the Bundt pan and bake for 1 hour, or until the top springs back when gently pressed and a tester inserted into the center comes out clean. Transfer to a wire rack and cool. Cut into slices and serve with a dollop of whipped cream.

# CHOCOLATE-GLAZED BACON BROWNIES

**MAKES 16 BROWNIES**

1/2 pound bacon, diced

1/4 to 1/3 cup butter, melted

2 (1-ounce) squares unsweetened chocolate

1 1/4 cups sugar

2 eggs

2 teaspoons vanilla

Pinch of salt

1/2 cup flour

1/2 cup heavy cream

1 cup semisweet chocolate chips

Preheat oven to 325 degrees. Prepare an 8 x 8-inch baking pan with nonstick cooking spray.

Cook bacon in a frying pan over medium heat until crisp. Remove and drain on paper towels, reserving pan drippings. Pour drippings into a measuring cup and add melted butter to make 1/2 cup; set aside.

Melt chocolate in a saucepan over medium heat and add the butter mixture. Remove from heat and stir in sugar until dissolved and combined. Beat in the eggs, vanilla, and salt. Fold in the flour and mix just until smooth.

Spread half the batter into the baking pan. Sprinkle half the bacon over batter and spoon remaining batter evenly over top. Bake for 30–35 minutes, or until a toothpick inserted into the center comes out clean.

Heat cream in a small saucepan over medium heat until simmering. Remove from heat and add chocolate chips; whisk until melted and smooth. Drizzle chocolate over the brownies and sprinkle with remaining bacon. Cool and cut into squares. Store in refrigerator.

# BACON WALNUT MAPLE FUDGE

**MAKES 64 PIECES**

1 cup packed dark brown sugar

1 (7-ounce) jar marshmallow crème

1 (5-ounce) can evaporated milk

6 tablespoons butter

1/8 teaspoon salt

1 (12-ounce) bag white chocolate chips

1 cup chopped walnuts

1 pound lean bacon, cooked and finely crumbled

1 teaspoon maple extract

Line an 8 x 8-inch baking dish with aluminum foil, leaving a 1-inch overhang on all sides; spray with nonstick cooking spray.

Combine brown sugar, marshmallow crème, milk, butter, and salt in a heavy saucepan. Cook over medium heat, whisking often, until mixture comes to a boil. Boil for 5 minutes, stirring constantly to prevent scorching.

Remove from heat and add the chocolate chips, stirring until fully melted and smooth. Stir in walnuts, bacon, and maple extract. Quickly pour into the pan and smooth the top. Refrigerate uncovered until firm, about 2 hours.

Use foil handles to lift fudge from the pan. Remove foil and cut fudge into 1-inch squares. Serve at once or store in an airtight container in the refrigerator.

# CHOCOLATE STOUT ICE CREAM

**MAKES 1 QUART**

4 ounces milk chocolate, finely chopped

4 ounces semisweet chocolate, finely chopped

1 cup milk

1/2 cup sugar

1/8 teaspoon salt

4 egg yolks

1 cup heavy cream

3/4 cup stout beer, such as Guinness

1 teaspoon vanilla

Put both of the chopped chocolates in a large bowl and place a mesh strainer over the top; set aside.

In a medium saucepan, combine the milk, sugar, and salt and bring to a boil over medium heat. In a medium bowl, whisk together the egg yolks. Slowly pour 1/2 cup of the milk mixture into the egg yolks, whisking constantly; add the warmed egg yolks back into the saucepan. Stir mixture constantly over medium heat until it thickens and coats the back of a spoon.

Pour the hot custard through the strainer over the bowl of chocolate, and stir until the chocolate melts. Whisk in the cream, beer, and vanilla. Let custard cool to room temperature, and then cover with plastic wrap and place in the refrigerator for at least 3 hours, or overnight. Freeze in an ice cream maker according to manufacturer's instructions.

# BACON PEANUT BUTTER COOKIES

**MAKES ABOUT 40 COOKIES**

1 pound bacon

2 ½ cups flour

½ teaspoon baking powder

½ teaspoon baking soda

½ teaspoon salt

½ cup butter, softened

1 cup packed dark brown sugar

1 cup sugar

1 cup smooth peanut butter (not natural)

2 teaspoons vanilla

2 eggs

1 ½ cups finely ground salted peanuts

Sparkling or raw sugar crystals, for sprinkling

In a large frying pan over medium heat, cook the bacon until crispy. Transfer to paper towels to drain; crumble into fine pieces. Allow the grease to cool in the pan for 5 minutes and pour through a strainer into a small bowl. Chill in the refrigerator for 30 minutes.

Heat oven to 350 degrees. Prepare a large baking sheet with nonstick cooking spray.

In a large bowl, combine the flour, baking powder, baking soda, and salt. In a medium bowl, beat the butter until creamy. Measure out 8 tablespoons of cooled bacon fat and add to the butter. Add the sugars, peanut butter, and vanilla; beat until creamy, 3–4 minutes. Add the eggs, one at a time, beating after each addition. Beat in the flour mixture to blend and add the ground peanuts and bacon until combined. Shape dough into 1 ¼-inch balls and place 2 inches apart on baking sheet. Dip a fork in warm water and flatten dough in a crisscross pattern. Sprinkle with sugar crystals. Bake until edges are just starting to brown, rotating halfway through baking, 10–12 minutes. Cool on sheet for 2 minutes before transferring to a wire rack.

# INDEX

# METRIC CONVERSION CHART

| VOLUME MEASUREMENTS | | WEIGHT MEASUREMENTS | | TEMPERATURE CONVERSION | |
|---|---|---|---|---|---|
| U.S. | METRIC | U.S. | METRIC | FAHRENHEIT | CELSIUS |
| 1 teaspoon | 5 ml | 1/2 ounce | 15 g | 250 | 120 |
| 1 tablespoon | 15 ml | 1 ounce | 30 g | 300 | 150 |
| 1/4 cup | 60 ml | 3 ounces | 90 g | 325 | 160 |
| 1/3 cup | 75 ml | 4 ounces | 115 g | 350 | 180 |
| 1/2 cup | 125 ml | 8 ounces | 225 g | 375 | 190 |
| 2/3 cup | 150 ml | 12 ounces | 350 g | 400 | 200 |
| 3/4 cup | 175 ml | 1 pound | 450 g | 425 | 220 |
| 1 cup | 250 ml | 2 1/4 pounds | 1 kg | 450 | 230 |

# ABOUT THE AUTHOR

Eliza Cross is the award-winning author of more than a dozen cookbooks, including the perennially popular *101 Things To Do With Bacon*. A food stylist, corporate recipe developer and marketing consultant, Eliza is also the founder of the bacon enthusiasts' society BENSA. She blogs about cooking, gardening and home ideas at Happy Simple Living and lives with her family in Denver.